DEBORAH LOCK has been writing and editing children's books and materials for over twenty years. She is the author of many DK Readers and Bible storybooks, and she is currently the publisher of Lion Children's Books in the UK. Passionate about singing, drama, and dance, Deborah is a licensed lay minister at her local church, where she leads worship and coordinates the yearly children-led Nativity service. She lives in England.

HELEN CANN is an illustrator, painter, and mapmaker based in England. She has illustrated more than twenty books, including *For Every Little Thing* (Eerdmans), *Manger* (Eerdmans), and *How to Make Hand-Drawn Maps* (Chronicle). Her work has appeared in exhibitions around the world and has been commissioned as props for film and television. Follow Helen on Instagram @helencannart or visit her website at helencann.co.uk.

First published in the United States in 2022 by Eerdmans Books for Young Readers,
an imprint of Wm. B. Eerdmans Publishing Co., Grand Rapids, Michigan
www.eerdmans.com/youngreaders

Text © 2020 Deborah Lock • Illustrations © 2020 Helen Cann
Originally published in the UK as *Prayers Around the World*
© 2020 Lion Hudson Ltd., Prama House, 267 Banbury Road, Summertown, Oxford OX2 7HT, England
www.lionhudson.com

Acknowledgments
All Scripture quotations, unless otherwise indicated,
are taken from the Holy Bible, New International Version®, NIV®.
Copyright ©1973, 1978, 1984, 2011 by Biblica, Inc.™
Used by permission of Zondervan.
All rights reserved worldwide.
www.zondervan.com.
The "NIV" and "New International Version" are trademarks registered
in the United States Patent and Trademark Office by Biblica, Inc.™
Psalm 148:7–12 taken from the International Children's Bible®.
Copyright © 1986, 1988, 1999 by Thomas Nelson.
Used by permission. All rights reserved.

30 29 28 27 26 25 24 23 22   1 2 3 4 5 6 7 8 9

ISBN 978-0-8028-5595-4 • **A catalog record of this book is available from the Library of Congress.**

Illustrations created with watercolor, collage, and colored pencil.

A World of Praise

DEBORAH LOCK

ILLUSTRATED BY HELEN CANN

EERDMANS BOOKS FOR YOUNG READERS

GRAND RAPIDS, MICHIGAN

*T*he earth is the Lord's, and everything in it,
the world, and all who live in it.

Psalm 24:1 – 2

*A*ll the world from East to West
gives praise to you.
We lift our voices,
we clap our hands,
we stamp our feet,
we dance, we sing,
we jump, we shout,
give praise to you.

All the world from North to South
gives praise to you.
All big things—
mountains and lakes,
waterfalls and volcanoes—
and all small things—
beetles and birds,
seeds and flowers—
give praise to you.

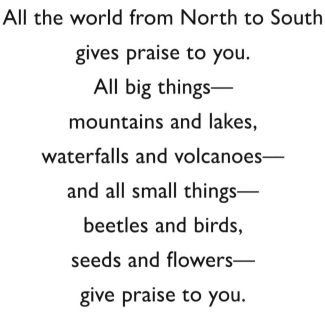

As the sun rises above tall peaks,
as colorful birds sing in the steamy jungle,
we take each new day with you.

Oh, the wonder of a new morning!

Oh, the warmth of the prairie breeze!

Oh, the sway of the ripening wheat!

Oh, the fullness of our daily bread!

Thank you for all that you provide

to fill our daily needs.

In the call of the condor,
over the peaks of the Andes,
in the whistle of the wind,
through the rush of the river,
in the warmth of the soil,
from the seed to a shoot,
your care flows in everything,
and all grows strong and plentiful.

You give new birth, new blooms.
You give joy within.
Over hill, over dale,
you spread hope within.
With friends, with family,
you shine love within.

From bustling cities
to shade of blossoming trees,
Lord, I seek your peace.

We thank you for our homes—
help us to be good neighbors.
We thank you for the countryside—
help us to care for plants and animals.
Like seeds scattering in the breeze,
help us to spread your love for all.

Beneath the pagoda, I look and listen.
You are everywhere and in everything:
in the song of a nightingale,
in the ripple of the koi,

in the shape of a gingko leaf,
in the crafted arch of the bridge.

The breeze rustles the palm leaves.

The sea whispers inside a conch shell.

Of what wonders do they speak?

They speak of you and your creation.

How you know each of us, just like

every grain of sand.

How we are more special and unique to you

than the great variety of shells.

How your love for us is far greater

than our understanding.

North wind blows,
seabirds swoop overhead.
Water laps over toes,
fish wriggle beneath.
Clouds drift by,
rain comes and goes.
Keep us safe in
your loving care.

Thank you for the harvest,
for all that you provide.
For sweet-tasting fruits from bush and tree,
in orchard, forest, farm, and field.
May we share your riches with one another.

Church bells ring out, welcoming all,
over the eaves where swallows nest.
Bicycle bells ring, trains toot, cars beep,
we go off to school through the busy streets.
Laughter rings out—it's time for fun.
Wrapped up warm, we kick the leaves.
Bless our homes, our work, and our play.

We come together for a time of thanksgiving.

We join together to support each other.

We meet together to share what you have given us.

We celebrate together with thanks to you.

For our food, our freedom, and our country.

Through the colors of the day
bring us joy and blessings.
Blue skies with fluffy white clouds,
green forests and fields of grass,
red rosy smiling faces,
yellow rays of sunshine,
pink petals, brown seeds,
oranges and purple grapes,
silver threads of spiders' webs,
golden falling leaves,
rainbows of sunlight through the rain,
fiery sunsets, and then black as night.

Long hours of daylight, then darkness reigns.
But in this land of ice and snow,
I am never alone.
You are with me, always.

Bwana, O Lord, shining light in the dark.

May peace be with us as we rest tonight.

God of far and wide, high and low,
great and small, stay close to us as we sleep.

The land yields its harvest;
God, our God, blesses us.

Psalm 67:6

From the rising of the sun to the place where it sets,
the name of the Lord is to be praised.

Psalm 113:3

*P*raise the Lord from the earth.
Praise him, you large sea animals and all the oceans.
Praise him, lightning and hail, snow and clouds,
and stormy winds that obey him.
Praise him, mountains and all hills,
fruit trees and all cedar trees.
Praise him, you wild animals and all cattle,
small crawling animals and birds.
Praise him, you kings of the earth and all nations,
princes and all rulers of the earth.
Praise him, you young men and women,
old people and children.

Psalm 148:7 – 12

Sunrise
INDIA

Wheatfield
UNITED STATES

Mountains
PERU

Hill and Dale
UNITED KINGDOM

Cherry Blossoms
JAPAN

Town and Country
GERMANY

Gardens
CHINA

Beaches
PACIFIC ISLANDS

Coastline
NORWAY

Street
ESTONIA

Harvest
CANADA

Cityscape
UNITED STATES

Leaves and Colors
NEW ZEALAND

Ice and Snow
GREENLAND

Moonlight
NEPAL

Savanna
KENYA